Problem Pe...

and how to

a quick ...

Ursula Markham

DANIELS
AN IMPRINT OF FOLENS

ISBN: 1 85467 317 3

© Printed 1995, 1996

Folens Publishers
Albert House
Apex Business Centre
Boscombe Road
Dunstable LU5 4RL
Tel: 01582 472788   Fax: 01582 472575

Foreword

I like the idea of Quick Guides. Teachers need reliable information and advice on a very wide range of subjects related to their work and they need it to be accessible and concise. This series attempts to meet those needs by drawing on the knowledge of experienced practitioners and presenting the essential material in a format which facilitates rapid reference and provides valuable action checklists.

I am sure that these guides will be useful to teachers, to governors, to parents and indeed to all who are concerned with the effective management of all aspects of education.

John Sutton
General Secretary
Secondary Heads Association

About the author

Ursula Markham is a hypnotherapist and counsellor
with a background in psychology. She conducts
seminars for large and small businesses, and has
broadcast and published widely in the field of
personal development.

Contents

Problem people and how to handle them: a quick guide

Introduction

Problem people are all around us. They are the ones who make life so difficult, either at work or in our personal lives. Some are deliberately difficult, others unconsciously so. The result is the same: they cause stress and annoyance, waste time and energy and can disrupt an entire project.

Of course, we can all be difficult at times, but some people are consistently so. Strictly speaking, it is their behaviour that is difficult, rather than the people themselves. In this booklet we will look at ways of dealing with the more common behaviour traits that cause us to see people as 'problem people'.

You cannot change another person, so problem people will remain problem people unless they themselves decide to do something about it. But you can use the techniques outlined in this book to change your response to them and reduce the stress and aggravation they cause.

The same techniques apply whether the problem person is a colleague, someone in a senior position, someone you have seniority over or someone you have occasional contact with. Or you may be called upon to mediate or advise in a situation that does not affect you personally. Whatever the circumstances, a certain amount of understanding, coupled with the necessary skills, will ensure that those problem people lose their ability to disrupt other people's lives.

A poor self-image

Feelings about oneself are formed in the very early years of life. There are many reasons why someone might feel inferior or insecure. Perhaps they had an over-strict upbringing, or perhaps an over-protective one. Either might leave the individual feeling that they are unable to cope alone. Sometimes it is circumstances, rather than anyone's actions, that cause the development of a poor self-image: many moves of home or changes of school, the loss or prolonged absence of a parent, or being brought up in an unsettled environment. Many people may experience these things and not be adversely affected, but for others they can produce a sense of inferiority and low self-esteem.

The life that followed

Someone who starts out in life with a poor self-image will usually have their sense of inadequacy compounded as the years progress. They often suffer from bullying, whether physical or emotional, because of their 'victim mentality'. Each unfortunate event simply serves to increase their belief that they are inferior and unworthy. Some people will collapse altogether and set a pattern for future failure in their lives. Others respond to such treatment with aggression, either overt or underhand and manipulative. Any of these may go on to become the difficult people with whom you have to deal.

What makes a problem person?
(continued)

Current problems

Everyone has to deal with problems throughout life. Some problems are great, some are small. Most of us cope with them fairly well. For someone with a poor self-image, however, or other problems in their life, a situation which anyone else would be able to cope with may seem greatly magnified. Each time such a person has to face a problematic situation, his or her sense of inadequacy is increased. Even if they actually succeed in coping with it quite well, they usually believe that they have been lucky and have 'got away with it', so there is no sense of pride or satisfaction in their achievement.

Change – even for the better – can be uncomfortable.

Fear of changing

For most people, no matter how dissatisfied they may be with themselves and their life, it is easier to continue in the same way than it is to make deliberate changes. Change, even change for the better, is never comfortable. Just as old shoes are more comfortable than new ones, old habits are more comfortable than making changes. If someone has grown to believe that they can only get what they want by being difficult, they will feel that to attempt any other approach would make them lose face before others. So they continue in the same negative fashion.

You cannot change other people, but you can learn to deal with them more effectively.

Accept that you cannot change anyone else

Only people who truly wish to change, and who make the effort to do so, can achieve change. Difficult people have discovered that the only way they can 'win', even if their victories are sometimes temporary and often hollow, is by being difficult; they see no reason to change. This being the case, the only thing you can change is yourself: your attitudes and your reactions. Direct confrontation is rarely the answer. It simply makes the difficult person dig their heels in still further and refuse to co-operate in any way.

Make the most of situations that present themselves

When dealing with a difficult person, you cannot expect to get everything you want from a situation. Even if you do not achieve one hundred per cent of what you wanted, if you are able to achieve most of it, in as short a time as possible and with as little disruption as possible, you should be pleased with yourself. Remember that avoiding the extreme stress of an awkward situation can be worth a great deal, as it reduces damage to the physical, mental and emotional well-being of all concerned.

Adjust your own behaviour

Learn to develop assertive behaviour, so that you are neither crushed nor angered by the situations a difficult person can cause. This may well be what they want: many difficult people only want to be the centre of attention. An assertive person accepts that the most satisfactory solutions call for a certain amount of compromise, and delights in situations where everyone wins to some extent and no-one loses completely.

You can learn how to adapt your own behaviour when necessary to become more assertive.

Realise that compromise is not the same as giving in

Many people believe that if they do not hold out for everything they want, they are being weak or submissive. This is not so. It shows a great deal of maturity and strength of character to be able to propose or accept compromise in cases where no principles are at stake.

Aggressive people are insecure; they try to bolster their own ego by always getting their own way.

The ways people behave can be divided into three main categories and, although we can all exhibit elements of each of them, most people conform predominantly to one or another. The three types are: aggressive, submissive and assertive. To deal satisfactorily with problem people, it is essential to be able to recognise each of these types, so that you can adjust your own behaviour accordingly.

Aggressive

The aggressive person is extremely selfish and determined to get their own way, even if it means hurting others. They have to be the winner in all situations, but their victories are only useful in the short-term; they inspire no loyalty and gain no friendship.

An aggressive person enjoys giving orders and telling others what to do, as this gives them the sense of power on which they thrive.

Someone who is aggressive will often have a lot of energy, and may well be good at what they do, but their behaviour will prevent them receiving the appreciation of others, either the people they hurt or bystanders who observe their tactics.

Although they would never admit it, an aggressive person is basically an insecure person: someone who is confident and has reasonably high self-esteem does not feel the need to be unpleasant to other people in order to get his or her own way. Anyone who is sure of themselves does not have to prove their power to others.

The individual who demonstrates such behaviour can be likened to the playground bully, who is basically insecure and often cowardly, usually picking on people who are least able to defend themselves. The school bully will strike out at their victim before they can themselves be hit and, in the same way, an aggressive adult will attack their victim before anyone else has the chance to question their own views or behaviour. The more critical they are of others, the more they boost their own self-image.

Demonstrations of aggression are a form of bullying.

How to recognise an aggressive person:

- Typical body language:
  - stands stiffly and rigidly
  - may keep their arms folded for much of the time
  - bangs furniture
  - points at the person to whom they are speaking, or makes stabbing gestures

- Typical phrases:
  - You must…
  - You'd better…
  - You're stupid!
  - I want you to…

Submissive

Submissive people have low self-esteem.

The submissive person is someone who always puts others first. This may sound a worthy trait but someone who is submissive takes it to extremes, seeming to encourage others to take advantage of them.

Like the aggressive person, the submissive person may also be insecure and lacking in confidence. This may cause them to become withdrawn and a loner: they may believe that others do not want their company. They may also feel that they do not deserve to be accepted by others and so they keep their distance.

This person, of course, makes the perfect victim for the aggressive person when they are looking for someone to pick on or to blame.

The submissive person will usually hide their deepest feelings. They may think they are acting as if everything is fine but, because they know inside that it is not, they believe themselves to be a fraud and thus dislike themselves even more. This causes them to become permanently stressed as they wait for others to catch them out and discover what a failure they really are.

Because of their low self-esteem, a submissive person is quite unable to accept a compliment. Praise them for a piece of work, and they will immediately point out to you the part that they had to correct. Compliment them on their clothes or their appearance and they will come straight back with a self-deprecating remark.

Most people begin by being quite sympathetic towards the submissive person; after all, they seem to need their company and even their protection. But eventually many people grow irritated with their behaviour and either become more aggressive than they would usually be or else leave them alone altogether.

Other people may become irritated with someone who is submissive.

How to recognise a submissive person:

- Typical body language:
  - head down – lack of eye contact
  - backs or leans away during conversation
  - nervous hand movements
  - speaks softly or in a whining tone

- Typical phrases:
  - I'm sorry.
  - Oh dear!
  - I wonder whether you would mind…
  - I'm sorry to bother you but…

Of course, the examples of the aggressive and submissive people given here are extreme, and most individuals will only exhibit a few of the given characteristics. However it is the extreme examples – and there are many of them – who are the problem people we have all the trouble with.

*An assertive
person cares for
herself or himself
and for others too.*

Assertive

The person who is assertive will not be a problem or cause you any particular difficulties. However, this is the third major type of behaviour and you should be able to recognise it whenever you are lucky enough to come across it. In addition, it is the type of behaviour we should all aim to use as much as possible.

An assertive person cares for themselves and for others too. They like nothing better than a 'win/win' situation. This is the only one of the three types of behaviour that usually achieves people's aims in the long term.

If someone is assertive, they do not necessarily think that they do everything right, but they are willing to accept this and to admit and put right any mistakes they do make. They have a positive self-image that enables them to respect themselves and others too.

How to recognise an assertive person:

  Typical body language:
  - posture is upright yet relaxed
  - able to maintain eye contact
  - always approachable

  Typical phrases:
  - What do you think?
  - I feel…
  - Let's…

Categories of problem behaviour

Everyone can be difficult from time to time; the ways in which people usually create problems can be divided into 12 basic categories. It is not possible to change people who cause problems by force of will, but it is essential to be able to deal with their behaviour so as to minimise the difficulties it can cause and protect everyone from undue stress and aggravation.

Critical

A person who takes a delight in belittling others. Sometimes the criticism will be specific (You look dreadful!), and sometimes it will be more general (You're hopeless!). They can make you feel really miserable. If you agree with them, they will think they have won; if you try and stand up for yourself or find fault with them, they will come back with even more criticism. This is a person who is basically insecure and the only way they know of building themselves up is by putting other people down.

What to do:

- Don't become either aggressive or submissive.
- Ask an assertive question: 'What makes you think that?' They will either not know what to say or will bluster; in either case they will have lost control of the situation.

The critical person delights in belittling others.

The unreliable person often means well; volatile people are unable to cope with pressure.

Unreliable

Someone who is never on time for an appointment and never gets work finished in time. A pleasant person who means well, they are so anxious to be liked that they take on more than they can manage, although they have good intentions at the time. As people get irritated with them, they become more anxious and promise even more.

What to do:
- Let them know that you enjoy their company or assistance (but only if you can do so sincerely).
- Ask for their opinion.
- When they offer to do something, check that they will be able to do it.

Volatile

This person can be charming one minute and then explode with rage, losing all control. They are quite unable to take pressure, as this adds to their existing feelings of inferiority. This is why they tend to attack before they can be attacked by others. This is someone it would be best to avoid altogether but, if this is not possible, there are some ways of avoiding trouble.

What to do:
- Keep quiet when they explode, maintaining eye contact until they run out of steam.
- Try to change the scene: suggest a walk or a cup of coffee to allow them time to cool down.
- Say that you would like to know what the problem is, and then offer help if appropriate.

Bullying

A highly aggressive person who will shout, point and bang the table. They want their own way at any cost. They will usually have a good mind and be capable of making quick decisions but, if those decisions are ever wrong, they will refuse to admit it.

What to do:
- Maintain eye contact and level (stand if they stand, sit if they sit).
- Don't become aggressive yourself; you will not beat them at their own game.
- When they interrupt, stop them and tell them that they are doing so.
- Tell them if you don't agree, but ask them to explain their thoughts.

Malicious

This is someone who talks about you behind your back, while making sure that what they say gets back to you. They won't worry too much about whether what they say is true or not. They also like to make jokes at other people's expense and, if the victims are not amused, they accuse them of having no sense of humour.

What to do:
- Get them alone so that they cannot 'play to the crowd'.
- Ask them whether they intended to be hurtful.
- Whatever their reply, suggest that they come to you with any criticisms in future.

Don't be aggressive with bullies: you're unlikely to win.

Thoughtless or unresponsive people do not usually set out to create difficulties.

Thoughtless

This person does not deliberately cause problems, but they tend to think of themselves and not other people. If they want to talk to you, they do so, regardless of whether you are free to listen or not. They are infuriating, but not unpleasant, so it is difficult to be rude to them.

What to do:

- Say you have something to discuss with them and arrange a time to do so.
- Show that you empathise with them.
- Warn them that they may not like what you have to say before you ask if they realise the effect of their behaviour.
- They will probably make an effort to change, but may find it difficult. See if you can help them in any way.

Unresponsive

This is someone who says nothing, hoping that everyone will eventually stop asking questions. This is frustrating and may make you angry. Sometimes this person is trying to exert power by keeping silent; sometimes they are simply frightened of saying the wrong thing.

What to do:

- You must get them talking, so start a conversation with something trivial and then ask an open question.
- If they do not respond, stay silent but maintain friendly body language.
- If there is still no response, comment on how ridiculous the situation is and ask what is on their mind.

Negative

Someone who always expects the worst in any situation. They can be very depressing to those around them. They do not come up with any ideas of their own, preferring to shoot down those of other people.

What to do:
- Ask them to be specific: what are their fears?
- Ask for a suggested solution.
- Ensure that you do not allow them to make you negative too.

Opinionated

Some people act in an opinionated fashion when they are right; this can be irritating enough. But the real problems arise when the opinionated person does not really know what they are talking about. They want other people's respect, so they lay down the law. If directly confronted, they can become vengeful and malicious.

What to do:
- Get them alone, so that they do not feel they are being made to look small in front of others.
- Express your view of the facts and make a comment to save them face ('Perhaps you were thinking of our other project').

Miserable

This person uses complaining words, often in a whinging tone. When things are wrong, they do not try to do any-thing, but complain to others they hope will sort it out. If they do not, the fault is theirs and not the complainer's.

Negative people can be depressing to those around them, and opinionated ones can be extremely annoying.

Try to get problem people on your side by talking to them.

What to do:

- Interrupt their flow as soon as possible.
- Paraphrase their main points and ask them what they think should be done (this will make them either stop and think or go away and leave you alone).

Procrastinating

A genuinely nice person who really wants to help but is so frightened of doing something wrong that they do nothing at all, hoping the situation will vanish. As other people grow tired of waiting and tackle the tasks themselves, it often does.

What to do:

- Ask what they are worried about and discuss possible solutions.
- Praise them when they have done something well.

Interfering

This person thinks that no one else is as good as they are. They delegate a task and then want to redo or check it themselves. This causes a backlog, so that many things are not done at all.

What to do:

- If you do a piece of work for this person, supply proof that you have done what you claim.
- Set deadlines for them, but give reasons for doing so or they will simply ignore them.

Dealing with conflict

Whatever the situation, a certain amount of conflict is going to be inevitable, as different people hold different opinions and have different temperaments; and this is not a bad thing. A destructive situation can arise, however, when conflict gets out of hand and involves personalities as opposed to situations or ideas.

Some conflict can have positive results, provided it is aims and ideals rather than individual personalities that are the subject.

Properly handled, conflict can have positive results.

- [ ] The discussion which ensues could bring to light one or more different solutions to an existing problem.
- [ ] It could encourage better communication among those involved.

Conflict that is not properly handled, however, can result in:

- [ ] People's thoughts becoming distracted from the main issues.
- [ ] Resentment, and therefore lack of co-operation, among those who are not happy with the outcome.

Try to understand the other person's point of view even if you don't agree with it.

How to resolve conflicts that involve you personally

- Recognise and consider the differences that exist and realise that each person involved has his or her own needs and expectations.

- If you find that you are frequently in conflict with certain people, try and understand both yourself and them and work out why conflict keeps arising.

- Take the time to listen to the views of others, even if you do not agree with them. Ask them to express themselves assertively, rather than aggressively. Having listened to them, request that they extend the same courtesy to you, making sure that you too remain assertive rather than aggressive.

- Try to understand their viewpoint, even if you do not agree with it. Realise that it is not possible for everyone to agree all the time and that it does not make either party superior if their view takes precedence or inferior if it does not.

- Once the conflict has been resolved, see if there is anything you can learn from it, to make it less likely to happen in the future.

How to resolve conflicts between others when you are not personally involved

☐ Whatever your own views on the topic, and which-ever of the parties you feel more sympathetic towards, it is essential to remain impartial if you are to avoid later resentment.

☐ Some people are naturally more able to express themselves than others, so be certain to allow everyone the same opportunity to speak.

☐ Prevent the situation from becoming heated; all reasonable discussion, even when ideas differ, can be productive

☐ If you feel it is necessary to tackle any individual about his or her attitude, do so in private. To do it in front of other people would not only be unfair but would create resentment.

☐ Whatever the outcome, try to summarise it in such a way that no one loses face.

All conflict causes a certain amount of stress.

Conflict and stress

All conflict, whether actual or anticipated, can be stressful. Once an individual is suffering from stress, the possibility of resolving conflict painlessly becomes more remote. Someone under stress is more likely to feel anger and frustration, and therefore to dig their heels in and refuse any sort of compromise.

Whether you are personally involved or mediating, the aim should be to persuade everyone to act in as asser-tive a way as possible. In fact, the more assertive (as opposed to aggressive) individuals are, the less likely it is that serious conflict will arise in the first place.

Good communication helps to avoid problems.

Good communication is a very important part of dealing with people and avoiding problems and difficulties in all aspects of life. It is the things which are either left unsaid or misunderstood that can cause people to become problem people.

Feedback is a vital part of good communication. It is never safe to assume that what has been said has been fully understood. If you insist on a response from the person you have been speaking to, you can find out whether they have understood what you have been saying. This will save time and will prevent bad temper on either part.

Feedback is not the same as repeating 'parrot-fashion' what you have heard: it is quite possible to do that without having understood the true meaning of the words. Any listener should be able to paraphrase what has been said and explain it in their own words, so that the original speaker feels confident that what they said has been understood. If it has not, this will soon become obvious to the speaker and they will be able to clarify their position.

If you are sending the message

You have to be aware not only of your words but also of the tone of your voice and your body language. In fact, it has been shown that only 7% of the message is understood by means of the words spoken, while 13% relies on the tone of voice and 80% is conveyed by the speaker's body language. It is up to you, therefore, to ensure that all these are compatible. If they are not, the listener will believe your body language rather than your words.

There are a number of points to bear in mind when conveying a verbal message:

- **The previous knowledge of your listener**. If you are the one conveying the information, you probably know more about the subject than the listener. Take care not to go too fast or to assume knowledge they may not have; this will only confound or confuse.

- **Ability to concentrate**. Not everyone has a long concentration span, so watch for signs of the listener's concentration fading.

- **Nervousness**. Many people are nervous when given important instructions or information, and may misunderstand or forget as a result.

Your body language conveys more than the words you speak.

Language problems. It will be obvious if you and the listener do not share a common first language, but, even if this is not the case, remember that some people experience difficulties with regional speech or technical terminology.

Distractions. The listener may be feeling unwell, or may have personal worries or shoes that pinch. Any such problems may cause lapses in attention.

Ability to retain what is said. Just as concentration varies, so does the ability to remember what has been heard. This is why feedback is so important.

There may be physical problems. The listener may have a hearing disability or other problems that stop them hearing or understanding you easily.

Making your point

Be assertive in speech and body language.

Watch the listener. You will soon become aware if they are failing to understand you or if their mind is elsewhere.

Be sure to use words and terminology they will understand.

Be as clear and concise as possible.

Ask for feedback and be prepared to listen to it, giving further explanation if you feel it necessary.

Body language

- reinforces the words you use and emphasises the message you are transmitting.
- gives the listener an indication of your state of mind.
- can sometimes replace a verbal message completely (think of a nod or a shake of the head).

If your body language is at variance with what you say, it:

- contradicts what you have been saying.
- can be misleading or confusing.

Keeping your body language assertive is extremely important if effective communication is to be achieved. It involves:

- maintaining eye contact.
- remaining relaxed throughout.
- keeping your gestures open and remembering to smile frequently.

Although body language is the greatest key to understanding the person you are dealing with, never be tempted to judge someone on a single aspect of their body language. Look for several to bear out your opinion; the listener could have a pain, or be suffering from a cold or affected by any number of factors you do not know about.

Keep your body language assertive.

*Learn to listen
actively.
Think about the
meaning behind
the words.*

If you are receiving the message

You need to listen actively, rather than let the sound
wash over you. You can prove that you are doing so to
yourself and to the other person by giving regular
feedback. This involves commenting on what has been
said, or paraphrasing it back to the speaker, so that
they know you have been following what they were
saying or, if you have misunderstood, they are
immediately aware of the fact. It is also necessary to
bear in mind the following.

☐ Concentrate. Do not only listen to the words
themselves but think about the meaning behind
them.

☐ Accept that, although you might not always agree
with the speaker, they have the right to their
opinions, just as you have the right to yours.

☐ Never think that you can anticipate what the
speaker is going to say next. Of course, you could
be right, but you might just as easily be wrong, and
then you might not catch what they really say.

☐ Listen to the speaker's intonation and watch their
body language.

☐ Give regular feedback, asking questions if there is
anything you do not understand.

How to say no

Saying no is very difficult for most people. It is hard enough when you feel that there is an obvious reason for doing so, but it is even worse if you simply do not wish to do something.

Stop and consider the alternative. Suppose you do not say no when you feel you should; what happens?

If it is a work situation:

- you will end up being the one given all the extra tasks or being asked to work unsocial hours.

If it is a social situation:

- you will probably be taken advantage of.

Whichever type of situation you are in, the result is likely to be that you will suffer from excess stress, which could prove harmful not only to your physical health but to your emotional well-being too.

Most people want to be helpful towards others whenever they can, but there are times when it is essential to set personal limits. It is better to do this at the outset, and say no, than to agree to something and find either that you are not able to do it or that you manage but end up feeling resentful towards the person who asked you.

Saying no is difficult, but everyone needs to be able to do it.

The work situation

Why people do not say no:

☐ They fear that the other person (perhaps a supervisor or even an employer) will be angry with them. Even if initially annoyed, a reasonable person will not be angry. Indeed, an employer is far more likely to be angry if your work is of a poor standard. Should the other person act aggressively, you have learned how to deal with that by being assertive.

☐ They do not want to appear either lazy or inefficient. This is unlikely to happen unless you have always shown yourself to be so. If you are a hard and efficient worker, that fact will have been recognised by others, even those who fail to comment upon it.

☐ They are frightened of losing their job. If you were to take on every task handed to you, and then found yourself unable to cope, you would almost certainly become stressed, which could lead to illness and time off work.

If you say no at the outset to tasks you feel you cannot cope with, you will gain the respect of those around you. In addition, it is possible that the person making the request did not realise that you were overburdened, and your refusal might make them understand better in the future.

The personal situation

You may not want to say no because you are afraid of losing a friend. But a real friend is not someone who takes advantage of you or who wants your friendship only for what they can gain by it. If someone is being unwittingly selfish, your refusal may make them more considerate in future. If someone is deliberately using you, they do not like you for yourself and have never really been a friend in the first place.

Consider each situation

Every situation needs to be looked at separately. While you may be ready to drop everything in order to take a non-driving friend to the doctor when an emergency arises, you will not necessarily be prepared to be called on to give lifts everywhere.

If you have always found saying no difficult, it could be that you are not assertive enough and need to work on enhancing your self-esteem. You might also need to consider your body language. How do you appear to others? Perhaps you give the impression of being submissive and therefore easily put upon.

You will never lose a true friend by saying no.

You have the right to say no. A simple explanation will be welcome, but there is no need for an excuse.

Saying no

- Consider the specific situation and make up your mind what you really want to do.
- If you feel that you need to know more about what the request entails, do not hesitate to ask for further details.
- If you then decide to say no to all or part of it, do so as soon as possible, remaining calm and assertive.
- It is not necessary to make excuses or tell lies. A simple explanation is sufficient, such as:
  - I make it a personal rule never to lend money.
  - I do not like Indian food.
  - I can't take on any more commitments just now.
- There is no need to apologise. If you always begin by saying 'I'm sorry but...', there are those who will try to manipulate you by playing on your feelings of guilt.

There will be times when you feel that you should say no to a particular request, but will still want to help the person concerned. In such a case, listen to what they say and give feedback so that they realise that you understand and care. Then say no, giving your reason, but see if you can help them find a different solution to the problem.

Remember, every human being has rights:

- The right to an opinion and to have their opinion heard.
- The right to say no when they feel it is justified.

As an assertive person, you can prevent these rights being abused. You will be able to deal far more effectively with potential problem people.

Complaints and complainers

It is very uncomfortable to find yourself on the receiving end of complaints, especially if they are not justified. Even those that are justified may not be your fault; it could be that you are just the initial contact. There is always a temptation in such cases to respond in a negative way, by justifying yourself, becoming defensive, getting angry or growing depressed. None of these will ease the situation.

However difficult it may be, the first rule is to stay calm. If everyone becomes angry, nothing can be achieved. Each of you will become stressed, which can lead to bad feeling and even physical ill effects. It is far easier to become heated than to calm down. If you lose your cool, the feeling is likely to stay with you and affect the way you interact with everyone you meet during the day.

If you receive a complaint, stay calm.

How to handle complaints:

☐ The first and most important thing is to relax, so take a deep breath and don't answer too quickly.
☐ There are three main types of complaint:
  - those that are justified
  - those where the person thinks they have a genuine grievance, but is mistaken
  - those that arise because the person enjoys complaining.
☐ Let the complainer go on with what they are saying. If you interrupt, they will probably start again from the beginning.

*If you are dealing
with complaints
face to face, keep
your body language
assertive.*

Face-to-face complaints

☐ Make sure your body language is assertive, that is,
maintain eye contact and use gestures that are
open and friendly. Let the person see you
listening: nod your head, or even make notes if
appropriate.

☐ Next, give some feedback indicating that you
understand their feelings (whether or not they are
right in their complaint). If the complaint is one
you cannot handle yourself, explain that you need
to check the facts and will let them know the
outcome of your investigations. Having said that
you will do this, it is essential that you do so.

☐ If you (or those you work with) are in the wrong,
apologise without making excuses and say what
you intend to do about it.

☐ If you are not certain how to go about putting
matters right, ask the complainer what they would
like to see done.

☐ If it is impossible to comply with their wishes, see if
you can find an alternative 'win/win' solution.

☐ Keep to the point. However aggressive the
complainer may become, remain calm and keep
bringing them back to the point. If you fail to do
this you may find that the situation becomes
personal and it will be more difficult to sort out
the problem.

Problem people and how to handle them: a quick guide

Complaints and complainers
(continued)

Telephone complaints

These are often more difficult to deal with. By the time they reach you, the complainer may already have been passed from one person to another, growing more impatient each time.

There are also some people who will not be aggressive face to face but lose their inhibitions when they are on the other end of the telephone. You cannot see their body language and they cannot see yours, so you have to rely on what you say to show them that you are being open and assertive.

Telephone complaints require special handling.

- It is even more important to remain calm in such circumstances. Speak slowly and calmly, make notes and tell them you are doing so.
- If you should need to interrupt the complainer, use their name. This will catch their attention.
- If you should need to leave the telephone to check your facts, ask the complainer whether they would prefer to hold the line or wait for you to call them back.
- Paraphrase what they have said to you and suggest what you might be able to do. Ask them if they accept this or whether they would prefer some other course of action.
- If you find that you are unable to deal with the matter, tell them that you will call them back. Make sure you do so, or get a more appropriate person to call.

A good leader is a good communicator.

You may be in authority either at work or in a personal situation. The most important thing for any leader is to be a good communicator, good at giving information and receiving it. The better everyone understands the situation, as well as what is expected of them and why, the more likely they are to co-operate.

It is also important to give credit to anyone who deserves it, and pass on praise received from elsewhere, rather than keeping it to yourself.

A group needs to be able to trust its leader, so it is vital never to betray any confidence. If you feel that it would be advisable to take a particular matter further, you must explain the situation to the person concerned and ask their permission to do so.

The tasks of a good leader

Delegating

Most people find this one of the hardest things to do, some because they feel that no one can perform a particular task as well as they can and others because they fear people will think they are trying to avoid work.

Delegation involves selecting someone you think will
be able to do the job, briefing them on what is
involved and then leaving them alone to do it. There
is naturally an element of risk involved, but this should
be minimised by making a good choice and then
giving clear instructions. If the task is particularly
complicated, explain the general concept and then
divide it into parts and explain each separately. Always
encourage feedback and questions.

Remember to allow extra time for someone who is less
experienced than you to complete a task, and try to
avoid putting them under pressure. Things you find
easy may appear more complicated to other people. If
there are real problems, you may need to arrange
some training or practice; this will help both of you
feel more confident.

Mediating

Differences of opinion may arise among the members
of the group. It is your task as leader to resolve these
differences, but you must not allow yourself to become
personally involved. Without jumping to conclusions,
ask each person about the problem, ensuring that
everyone has a fair share of time to put whatever
points they choose. Although you may empathise
more with one person than another, you must be fair
and you must be seen by all to be fair.

Delegating is often difficult, but it is always important.

A leader must be seen by all to be fair.

Counselling

You should take a genuine interest in each member of your group, even though you will relate better to some than to others. It is your job to help each person develop self-confidence, and you can do this by listening to them, empathising with them and giving positive feedback. Sometimes you will be able to offer advice but, should an occasion arise when you are not able to, offer to find someone who will be able to help.

Empowering

It is the leader's task to motivate the group. If this is not done well, there will be no loyalty and the group's morale will deteriorate. Everyone needs to know that they are valued. Acknowledge the individual who has made the effort to do something well. Let them know that their efforts are appreciated.

Once you have explained what is wanted, stand back and let the group perform the task. They will know that you trust them and their confidence will grow as they complete more tasks successfully. While you should be available if needed, you must not appear to stand over them.

There is often at least one problem person in any group. Keep your eyes open for this: take them to one side and talk to them. Failure to do so will disempower the other members of the group.

Problem people a leader may have to deal with

Aggressive people

Although these people have an unfortunate manner, they are often capable and efficient. They need to know where they fit in and the significance of their tasks.

- Explain what is expected of them and why. Listen to any feedback, as they often have good ideas.
- Encourage them to feel part of the team as a whole.
- Acknowledge their achievements.

People who resist change

- Make a list detailing the proposed changes and setting out the pros and cons of each, and give it to them in advance.
- Bring everyone together and discuss the list, taking note of any objections. Try to put their minds at rest without trivialising their anxieties.
- Emphasise the benefits the changes will bring.

Regular absentees

- See whether you can discover the cause. Perhaps there are health problems, or maybe they are absent on the same day every week or every time they are faced with a particular task.
- Do what you can to encourage a sense of team spirit so that they feel they are part of the group.
- Talk to them about their absences so that they know you are aware of the situation. Ask if they would like to discuss their problems with you. If they would prefer to speak to an outsider, offer to find the appropriate professional.

Encourage a sense of team spirit

A good leader takes overall responsibility but gives others credit for what they do.

Time wasters

Some people waste time deliberately when they want to avoid certain tasks. Others are just well-meaning people who easily become sidetracked.

- If it is a commercial situation, ensure that they are aware that time is money. Even at school or home, other people will have to do more as a result.

- Point out that they are being unfair to other people.

- List the personal consequences if they do not sort themselves out: perhaps they will not have the opportunity to do things they really enjoy.

A good leader will

- Involve other people at every stage.

- Encourage feedback from those around them.

- Take overall responsibility while giving group members credit for their contribution.

Useful Addresses

British Association for Counselling (BAC)
1 Regent Place
Rugby
Warwickshire CV21 2PI
telephone 01788 550899
information line 01788 578328 (recording)

Changeworks
42–44 Brook Street
Warwick CV34 4BL
telephone: 01926 419650
(offers training in Neuro-Linguistic Programming, a
technique for exploring human communication)

Youth Access
Magazine Business Centre
11 Newarke Street
Leicester LE1 5SS
telephone 0116 255 8763
(National Association of Young People's
Counselling and Advisory Services)

Redwood Women's Training Association
20 North Street
Middleton
Manchester M24 6BD
telephone 0161-643 1986
(assertiveness training)

Bibliography

Elwood N Chapman, *Improving Relations at Work*, Kogan Page 1989.

D Mackenzie Davey, *How to be a Good Judge of Character*, Kogan Page 1989.

Helga Drummond, *Managing Difficult Staff*, Kogan Page 1990.

Gerard Egan, *You and Me: the Skills of Communicating and Relating to Others*, Brooks Cole 1977.

Rennie Fritchie and Maggie Melling, *The Business of Assertiveness*, BBC Books 1991.

Herbert S Kindler, *Managing Disagreement Constructively*, Kogan Page 1988.

Gael Lindenfield, *Assert Yourself*, Thorsons 1987.

Ursula Markham, *How to Deal with Difficult People*, Thorsons 1993.

Richard Nelson-Jones, *Lifeskills: a handbook*, Cassel 1991.

Gloria Steinem, *Revolution From Within: a book of self-esteem*, Bloomsbury 1992.

Anni Townend, *Developing Assertiveness*, Routledge 1991.

Manchester Open Learning Organisation, *Handling Conflict and Negotiation: a Management Guide*, Kogan Page 1993.

Developing Assertiveness Skills 2nd edition
Chrissie Hawkes-Whitehead
ISBN 1 85467 212 6

The Assertiveness Game
Eliot Franks
ISBN 1 85467 183 9

Power in the Workplace
Maureen LaJoy
ISBN 1 85467 193 6

Body Language
Ursula Markham
ISBN 85467 165 0

Active Listening: A Counselling Skills Approach
Anthea Millar and Angela Cameron
ISBN 1 85467 186 3

Raising Self Esteem: 50 Activities
Murray White
ISBN 1 85467 231 1

Self Esteem: Its Meaning and Value in Schools A and B
Murray White
ISBNs 1 85467 141 3 and 1 85467 142 1

Folens resource packs are:

✓ **Fully photocopiable**

✓ **Ready for use**

✓ **Flexible**

✓ **Clearly designed**

✓ **Tried and tested**

✓ **Cost-effective**

The Quick Guide series from Folens

Quick Guides are up to date, stimulating and readable A5 booklets, packed with essential information and key facts on important issues in education.

Health education

Drugs Education for children aged 4–11: A Quick Guide
Janice Slough
ISBN 1 85467 326 2

Drugs Education for children aged 11–18: A Quick Guide
Janice Slough
ISBN 1 85467 324 6

Alcohol: A Quick Guide
Dr Gerald Beales
ISBN 1 85467 300 9

Smoking Issues: A Quick Guide
Paul Hooper
ISBN 1 85467 309 2

Sex Education: A Quick Guide for Teachers
Dr Michael Kirby
ISBN 1 85467 228 2

Sex Education for children aged 4–11: A Quick Guide for parents and carers
Janice Slough
ISBN 1 85467 312 2

Sex Education for children aged 11–18: A Quick Guide for parents and carers
Janice Slough
ISBN 1 85467 313 0

Career enhancement

Assertiveness: A Quick Guide
Chrissie Hawkes-Whitehead
ISBN 1 85467 305 X

Counselling: A Quick Guide
Chrissie Hawkes-Whitehead
and Cherry Eales
ISBN 1 85467 302 5

Problem People and How to Handle Them: A Quick Guide
Ursula Markham
ISBN 1 85467 317 3

Class and school management

Bullying: A Quick Guide
Dr Carrie Herbert
ISBN 1 85467 323 8

School Inspections: A Quick Guide
Malcolm Massey
ISBN 1 85467 308 4

Grief, Loss and Bereavement: A Quick Guide
Penny Casdagli & Francis Gobey
ISBN 1 85467 307 6

Safety on Educational Visits: A Quick Guide
Michael Evans
ISBN 1 85467 306 8

Equal Opportunities: A Quick Guide
Gwyneth Hughes & Wendy Smith
ISBN 1 85467 303 3

Working in Groups: A Quick Guide
Pauline Maskell
ISBN 1 85467 304 1

Organising Conferences and Events: A Quick Guide
David Napier
ISBN 1 85467 314 9

Working with Parents: A Quick Guide
Dr Michael Kirby
ISBN 1 85467 315 7

For further information

For further details of any of our publications mentioned in this Quick Guide, please fill in and post this form (or a photocopy) to:

Folens Publishers   Tel: 01582 472788
Albert House   Fax: 01582 472575
Apex Business Centre
Boscombe Road
Dunstable LU5 4RL

Name ....

Job Title ....

Organisation ....

Address ....

....

Postcode ....

Tel No. ....

Fax No. ....

☐   **Please send me details of the following publications:**

Notes

Problem people and how to handle them: a quick guide